SPEED READING
How to Read Fast, Faster

By Basil Foster

FREE DOWNLOAD

INSIGHTFUL GROWTH STRATEGIES FOR YOUR PERSONAL AND PROFESSIONAL SUCCESS!

My friends and colleagues Joshua Moore and Helen Glasgow provided their best seller on personal and professional growth strategies as a gift for my readers.

Sign up here to get a free copy of the Growth Mindset
book and more:
www.frenchnumber.net/growth

TABLE ON CONTENTS:

—

Introduction
Welcome to the Club ~ the Beginning of Your Speed Reading Journey

Greetings, readers! I want to thank you for purchasing this book, and my hope is that you will gain much wisdom from it. You will learn some great strategies, many of which have been scientifically proven to accelerate your reading capability.

Reading is a vital skill necessary for everyday communication. You have probably been reading for many years, but even though you can read there is still plenty of room for improvement.

By learning to speed read, not only will you become more knowledgeable, you will also enhance your communication skills.

Before you delve into this book, I recommend that you take the following two short surveys to give yourself a better idea of your reading capabilities. This will assist you in learning which areas you need the most improvement.

Why do you want to improve your reading?

Tick/highlight what you would like to gain from studying this book:

[] Increase the speed of my reading.
[] Use more effective strategies to save time.

[] Locate information quickly.
[] Get the main idea of a book.
[] Get the main idea as well as the detail of a book.
[] To read more effectively and efficiently.
[] To synthesize the information in a range of sources.
[] A better understanding of what I am reading.
[] To learn to apply information I have read.
[] To better articulate the information I have read.
[] To quickly become an expert reader.
[] To improve my concentration.
[] To stay motivatcd while I am reading.
[] To feel confident in my reading ability.
[] To read critically instead of accepting everything I read.
[] To ignore information that's not useful.
[] To increase my vocabulary.
[] To pass my exams.
[] .... (Anything not included in the list)
[] .... (Anything not included in the list)

Where are you now?

Before you start learning the speed reading techniques in this book, you might want to think about your current reading skills. Highlight/tick the statements in both the lists that describe the kind of reader you are. There are no right or wrong answers here; just go with your first reaction. The most important thing is the opinion that you have of yourself. Through this list you will learn things about yourself that will help you to become a better reader.

List 1

[] I am not a good reader.
[] I don't like reading; I always leave it to the last minute.
[] Reading makes me feel overwhelmed when I see how much I need to read.
[] I read very slowly.
[] I don't like marking or writing in my books.
[] If I don't read a book from cover to cover, I feel as if I'm going to miss something.
[] No matter what I'm reading I always read in the same way.
[] I get worried that I won't remember what I have read.
[] I get too engrossed in the details before I have understood the bigger picture.
[] I suspect that I'm dyslexic.
[] I want to improve my reading skills.
This book will help you if you can relate to any of these descriptions.

List 2

[] I love to read.
[] I read all the time.

[] I find it easy to locate key information.

[] I use a range of different techniques to read different material.

[] I am acquainted with the 80/20 rule and I apply it when I am reading.

[] I am confident, ignoring any information that is not relevant to what I need to know.

[] I can decide quickly whether a book is useful to me or not.

[] I know the difference between a good and a bad book as soon as I begin to read it.

[] I use certain strategies to remember what's important to me.

[] Before I start reading I know the reason why I'm doing so.

If you ticked more than 8 of these descriptions you already have a natural speed reading ability. However, this book will still be of great help to you and you will find that you will learn plenty of new techniques to better improve your speed reading skills.

Chapter 1
Understanding the Basics of Speed Reading

Reading is something that we do every day; on the job, at school, at home, there is always going to be information that you will need to read. Therefore, it's a very important skill to have and it's rather unfortunate that there are 115 million illiterate youths in the world today. You should really count yourself lucky that you know how to read at all, and be even more grateful that you can take your reading to the next level.

One of the definitions of the word "read" according to the Britannica encyclopaedia is "the input of information through written material." When you read you are transferring the information from the paper into your mind. If you have ever wondered why some people are more intelligent than others, it's not because they were born that way, it's because they read a lot. The more information you take in, the more you can put out. This is where it becomes important to have the ability to read more information in less time. This is also the difference between learning to read and reading to learn!

Bookworms worldwide get excited knowing that there is way that they can increase the speed of their reading. There are some people who have a reading list a mile long and just looking at that list can be overwhelming. The majority of people are capable of reading between 200 and 400 words per minute (wpm). This is the average amount of time it takes to read the information; for the brain to process it phonetically and then get a mental image of what we have read.

What if I told you that by practicing a few simple techniques you could read up to five times as fast as the average person? Being able to read 500 wpm would enable you to read 2 books per month as opposed to one book per month. Conventional reading causes our eyes to travel from left to right as we read each word in sequence. The optimal recognition point (ORP) is a point that is found near the center of the word. When your eyes locate the ORP, your brain starts processing the entire word and what it means within milliseconds. Your eyes keep following each word in the sentence until they come together to form a complete sentence. When your eyes meet punctuation marks, your brain is reminded to form a coherent thought. Your eyes will continue to glide over sentences until you have completed the book.

How we Understand Reading

The majority of people assume that reading involves continuously gliding your eyes over the lines on the page, reading the words individually, spelling them out syllable by syllable at the same time as silently sounding them out in your head. This faulty perception of the reading process is due to what we were taught as children. According to Tony Buzan there are two different techniques that teach people how to read. They are as follows:

1. **The phonetic method:** This is when each letter of the alphabet is pronounced and then the tones are combined to form a word.
2. **The see and say method:** This involves showing children an image and telling them to describe what they are looking at.

Both of these methods mean that when a child starts to read alone, the first thing they do is say the word in their head first before saying it out loud. This process is referred to as sub vocalization.

How Reading Concepts are Misunderstood

We make the assumption that our children can read when they can read alone without saying the words out loud. This is a very slow method of learning how to read and it carries over into adulthood. This is why the average person is only capable of reading 250 wpm, a university or college student might be capable of almost doubling that number to 400 wpm simply because they have so much information that they need to take in. However, if a person is trained how to speed read they can read up to 1000 words per minute, and if you really want to become an expert speed reader you can increase that number to 3800 words per minute.

I am almost certain that some of you are thinking that reading that fast is going to limit your ability to understand the text. This is not true at all; reading syllable to syllable is basically a waste of time and energy. Evelyn Wood is a speed reading expert, and she believes that the average person thinks at a speed of 5000 wpm. If you think at 5000 wpm but read at 250 wpm isn't it logical that you are still going to be able to understand the information when you are speed reading? This is why the majority of students get frustrated and bored when they are reading because their thinking speed is faster than their reading speed. To make matters worse, a lot of text contains so many unnecessary extra words that you end up taking in a lot of information that isn't needed. As a matter of fact, the message would make more sense without those added words.

Fun Fact: People only learned how to read in silence recently! This means that prior to this date we were only capable of reading out loud. So I'm assuming that libraries of the past didn't post "NO TALKING" signs! It must have been pretty loud.

The Correct Reading Application

A good reader is not someone who is capable of sounding out letters and combining them together to form a word. There is much more to true reading, such as having a full understanding of the text and being able to critically analyze it. According to Buzan, there are a number of different phases to the reading process, and if you want to improve your reading it is a necessity that all these phases are mastered.

1. **Recognition:** Recognizing the symbols of the alphabet.

2. **Assimilation:** This is the physiological process of reading and it involves the word reflecting light, being received through the eye and then passing through the optic nerve to the brain.

3. **Intra-integration:** This is the basic understanding of reading where different parts of the information are connected.

4. **Extra-Integration:** When knowledge previously gained is connected to new information being learned.

5. **Retention:** The process of the brain storing the information read.

6. **Remembering:** The ability to gain access to the information that has been stored.

7. **Communication:** This involves contemplating the information you have learned and having the ability to talk, write, and visualize this information.

The Way Language is Processed by the Brain

Reading has never been a natural process:

language was created by humans approximately 150,000 years ago. The alphabet is between 4,000 and 5,000 years old and according to a researcher at Oxford University in England, it's highly unlikely that during this time our brains have evolved enough to become reader friendly. The disadvantages of trying to train our brains to learn a new reading strategy are similar to trying to teach an old dog new tricks. The alphabet hasn't been around long enough to study how we've mastered it. When a new skill is developed, the brain's connective nerves create new highways to carry information. This makes us more adept, efficient and better at that particular skill. By making the transition to ORP style of reading, we could potentially weaken the muscles in the brain already developed over the thousands of years we've been reading.

In 2009, researchers at the Georgetown University Medical Center discovered that the cells required in the brain for word processing were on the left side of the brain. In other words, no one has a dictionary in their brain; evolution hasn't blessed us with this. The words have to be input and over time, humans gather words that are stored in this part of the brain. The left visual cortex of the brain is responsible for memorizing and processing the meaning of words. These words are then turned into whole units such as emotions, neighbours, dogs, siblings and trees etc.

The Advantages of Speed Reading

Speed reading isn't just about reading faster, it's about being better able to comprehend the information and to retain it. There are also many other benefits associated with speed reading. They are as follows:

Better Memory: If you train the brain it will grow stronger and perform better. It is very similar to a muscle. Speed reading challenges the brain to perform better, at a higher speed and at a higher level. When the brain is trained to take in information at a faster rate, one of the by-products is that there will be an improvement in other areas of your brain such as memory. When you read, your memory acts like a stabilizer muscle that is activated when you speed read.

Improved Focus: The majority of people have the ability to read approximately 200 wpm. This is the average reading speed. However, there are some people who are capable of reading up to 300 wpm. Why is there such a large gap? There are two main reasons for this:

1. The way we are taught to read as children is very inefficient.
2. The inability to focus.

When we are not able to focus on what we are reading, the mind wanders and becomes preoccupied with other thoughts. Speed reading will help you to improve your ability to focus.

Improved Self-Confidence: When you know that you can learn anything you want in a short space of time, you are naturally going to become more confident. When you are capable of learning more information, the doors of opportunity will start to open for you and your chances of succeeding in everything that you do will increase.

Improved Logic: When the brain is trained to read faster, it improves its ability to sort out information as well as find links between information that has been previously stored. The more the speed of your reading improves, the quicker this process happens and you will start to notice that problems that would usually take you a significant amount of time to solve are resolved in a much quicker time.

Here is a table of how speed reading benefits students of all levels.

	Average Reader	Speed Reader
Words per minute	200-300	600-1200
Comprehension	Has to read over the text several times	Even if the text has to be re-read it is done at a faster speed
Memory recall	Unable to focus due to the length of time it takes to read,	Extreme focus for short periods of time greatly improves

	therefore memory is poor	memory
Banal and boring material	Will fall asleep	Get it over and done with quickly
Theoretical textbooks	Unable to get to the main issues because of a lack of focus	Quickly gets to the central points and has a better understanding of the information
Dyslexic students	Avoids reading because they struggle	Improves reading speed by 500%
Lazy students	Don't read what they are supposed to	Read what they have to because they can do so quickly
Top students	Read instead of socializing	Get their reading done and have time to socialize
Mature students	Find it difficult to keep up with the extensive amount of	Get through all of the reading material and still have time to review for their exams

	reading material	
Athletes	Don't get the best grades because they are training	Can read everything they need to; get good grades as well as train
Bad students	Suffer from inconsistent grades	Are smarter than their friends because they can read faster
Parents	Give up trying to help their children get good grades	Can encourage their children to get better grades by teaching them to speed read
Business people	Miss key principles because they skim and skip their reading material	Capable of reading all of their material so their decisions don't suffer and neither do their careers

When Not to Speed Read

As you have read, there are several advantages associated with speed reading. However, there are situations when it is advised that you read at a slower pace. Here are some situations when it would be necessary to read slowly.

- **Reading Legal Documents**: Reading documents such as legally binding contracts should be read at a normal speed. In such an instance you are not trying to work out the key concepts, you want a thorough understanding of every word that you are reading. It can be tempting to speed through such documents because they can contain a significant number of pages. There are some words and phrases in legal documents that are not used in general conversation. Y

- You may need to stop and look these words up to get a better understanding of the information. Since you are going to be affixing your signature to the information, it is essential that you have a full understanding of what you are reading.

- **Literary pieces:** Literature such as novels and poems should be read at a normal speed, because they are not easy to understand. They also contain words and phrases that are not used in everyday language. Therefore, to read these words and phrases in context you are going to have to read slower.

- **Letters:** Letters received from significant people in your life such as friends and family members should not be speed read.

These letters are typically filled with emotion and you want to be able to feel what they are trying to communicate with you.

- **Instructions:** This applies particularly to electrical equipment or guides on how to assemble objects. You don't want to miss any key elements and end up injuring yourself or building a faulty item.

Speed Reading Myths

The assumption is that speed readers are just staring at the page and turning it after a couple of seconds. Some people believe that it's impossible to read and understand information at such a fast speed. Due to the fact that traditional education systems have conditioned us to read in a certain way, there are some people who simply don't believe this is possible. If you are one of those people or you know anyone who thinks this way I want to convince you that speed reading is a legitimate skill with many benefits.

Myth No. 1: Slow reading means better comprehension

It is a misperception that reading at a slower pace leads to better comprehension of the material being read because you are concentrating more. Although there are some exceptions, as you have just read, this is definitely not the truth in all cases. Concentration has nothing to do with how much you focus on one word: instead, it is about the how much your brain can handle at the speed that you are reading. When you read slowly it actually interrupts your ability to concentrate because you are focusing on one word at a time as opposed to a group of words which requires more concentration. This can then translate into less concentration.

Myth No.2: Speed readers just skip words

There is a misconception that speed reading is only possible because the reader is skipping words. The belief is that the words that are not important in the sentence are skipped. Once again, this is not the truth. Speed readers read each word on the page, even words such as articles and prepositions which are not considered important. The difference between a speed reader and a traditional reader is that they read words in groups. Hence their ability to read quickly.

Myth No. 3: Traditional readers enjoy what they are reading more

As we have mentioned there is some material that you should read at a normal pace. However, this doesn't apply to all material and it can actually make reading more enjoyable if you have the ability to speed read. Think about it like this. When you are reading fast the images are formed in your mind at a faster rate so it's almost as if you are watching a film in your mind. Traditional reading causes the images to appear in your mind in slow motion because they are only formed at the rate they are read.

Chapter 2
Speed Reading Preparation

Now that you have become more acquainted with speed reading, it's time to actually learn how to implement the skill. However, it isn't something that you are just going to dive into. You need to prepare your mind for the transition that is about to take place. Here are some preparation techniques.

Choose a Practice Book

The practice book is going to be your standard measuring tool; it will help you to judge your improvement as you practice your speed reading skills. The book you choose should be one that is relatively simple and that you can easily understand.

Your Baseline Reading Speed (wpm)

You need to have something to measure your improvement against. This means that you are going to have to count how many words you are capable of reading per minute.

- Use your practice book and time how many words you can read in one minute. This is a simple technique, set your timer for one minute. Start reading from the top of the page and mark the last word that you read. Once the timer stops, count the words that you have read and write the number down.

- Decide on a clear reading goal about what you want to accomplish when you are reading the material. Are you interested in the main plot of the story? Are you interested in analyzing the characters? Do you want to find the main message in the story? Whatever it is, make sure that you are clear about it. When you have a specific objective in mind, it makes it easier to easily find what you are looking for.

- You can't expect to enhance your speed reading skills if you don't practice consistently. Therefore, you are going to need to set a specific time every day to practice. The time when your brain is the most fertile is the early hours of the morning. You might not be able to set a time first thing in the morning, so just choose a time that's most convenient for you. Practicing your speed reading skills for 30 minutes per day will greatly enhance your ability to speed read.

- Depending on the type of content you want to read you can prioritize it into categories such as high and low attention. At this pointed, pre-reading becomes useful; however, we will get into this in the next chapter. It is up to you what order you decide to read the material in. Some people read high first and low second or vice versa; however, it is recommended that you read the high material first and low second.

- You need to concentrate when you are reading, even if you like reading with music or the TV on when you are practicing to speed read, you should turn it off. You want to make sure all distraction is eliminated; if you live in a noisy environment you can purchase a pair of earplugs to keep the noise out. Getting rid of distractions is very important because they can make you lose your focus, forcing you to start from the beginning.

- Don't wait until you are exhausted before you take a break; take one automatically every 10 minutes. This will give your eyes and brain time to relax before getting back to your practice. It's important that you take regular breaks because speed reading requires that you use rapid side to side eye movement as well as using your brain to process information faster, all of which is physically and mentally draining. With each break that you take, make it a habit to drink a glass or two of water because the brain depends on water in order for it to function properly.

When you are on a break, you will also need to get up, stretch and move around. Physical activity will help to eliminate drowsiness which can be common when people are reading.

- Speed readers have a wider vision range than readers who don't. This is because of their peripheral vision. You can enhance your vision range through certain eye exercises; you will learn about them in an upcoming chapter.

Chapter 3
Speed Read Pre-Read

A basic skill required by speed readers is the ability to pre-read information before actually reading it in its entirety. There are several benefits associated with pre-reading, they are as follows:

Pre-read Benefits

- **Improved Comprehension:** Pre-reading information enables you to better comprehend what you are reading. This is particularly true when reading difficult material. Pre-reading enables the reader to extract important information from the material being read so that when it actually comes to speed reading you already have a general idea of what the information is about. All you will need to do is find other information that can be combined with the information you have retained from the pre-read.

- **Faster Reading:** We know that speed readers can read faster than non-speed readers. However, this speed is increased with pre-reading. When you pre-read you come across the areas that are slightly more challenging, this means that you can do some research and get a better understanding before you actually start speed reading.

Pre-reading Methods

Pre-reading is a simple concept, and it isn't difficult to understand and apply. However, there are different methods which each have their own purpose. These methods are as follows:

Skimming: This is a specific form of pre-reading and it involves getting the general idea of each chapter in the book. Follow these steps in order to skim read effectively:

- Read the introduction. A good place to start is with the title and the opening sentence. These sections are direct and to the point, meaning that the reader is able to get a good idea of what to expect in the main body of the material.
- Read the subheadings. This is particularly important if the topic or chapter is divided into different paragraphs. It also demonstrates how each subheading relates to the main material.
- Look for technical terms and unusual words that you wouldn't use in everyday language. You can then look up the definitions to give you a better understanding of the text.
- Pay attention to information written in list form. Such material is often important and requires that you memorize the information.

- Skim information that answers the following questions: What happened? Where did it happen? How did it happen? And why did it happen? You should also look for superlatives such as the best or worst scenarios.

- To skim effectively you will need to read the first few sentences of each paragraph. This is where the main topic is typically located. The sentences will give you a clear idea of what the rest of the paragraph is about because sometimes the subheading will not give you enough information.

- Read the entire last paragraph because it will provide a brief description of everything that was written in that chapter.

Scanning: Another pre-reading method is a bit more specific than skimming and this is scanning. The main aim of scanning is to search for a single or a few pieces of information in the text. This means that you are not going to be reading different sections within the text. Your main focus is to find the specific piece of information that you are looking for and ignore everything else. You can scan effectively by following these tips:

- Don't waste your time looking at chunks of information. What you are looking for may be found represented by symbols or in a diagram.

- Always have a goal in mind of what you want to search for. This will make you more alert when you are scanning for the information, enabling you to easily find what you are looking for because you will be expecting it.
- If the material that you are reading is lengthy, you will need to focus on the subheadings for guidance as they will provide you with a brief idea of the main theme of the paragraph.
- Once you have found the information that you are looking for, make sure that you read the sentences directly after the subheadings. This will confirm whether or not you have found the information that you are looking for.

Previewing: If you want an idea of the general content of the text, previewing will help you to achieve this. This is particularly useful if the material that you are reading is of a long length. The main aim of the preview method is to tell you what the text is about. There are certain strategies you will need to follow in order to preview effectively, they are as follows:

- Search for keywords. A good author will make it clear what the information is about because s/he doesn't want it to be mistaken for another subject. Keywords also provide the reader with a general idea of what s/he can expect from the text. The majority of the keywords can be found in the summary or the Meta description, the subheadings, chapter or the title of the book. These will all provide you with a guide as to the contents of the book. This will help you to specify which sections of the book you are going to focus on.

- Look for key sentences. The majority of material is going to have a key sentence: this is also referred to as a "topic sentence." Due to the fact that all materials is written with a certain structure, it is not difficult to find the keywords. If the text is divided into a number of subheadings or paragraphs, you should expect that each paragraph is going to have a different key sentence. You should also note that the most important information in a paragraph or a subheading is always located at the beginning, because this provides the reader with what s/he should expect from that particular text. The final section provides a summary of the entire paragraph.

- Graphs, pictures, names, or numbers and enhancements within the text such as quotes, italics, and underlining are also important information points that you should be looking for when previewing.

- Pre-reading has similarities to surveying because it helps you to work out which parts of the text are important and require your attention. When you are familiar with the material that you are pre-reading it will help you to have a better understanding of the information that you are about to speed read. It will also help you to locate the information that you are looking for within a shorter space of time.

Chapter 4
Improve Your Vision
Through Eye Exercises

We read with our eyes, so if you want to develop your speed reading capabilities you are going to have to train your eyes to become capable of recognizing more words.

Peripheral Vision

Your peripheral vision is your ability to look at objects other than the ones that you are directly focused on. We typically fix our eyes on what's in front of us but we can also focus on what's going on around us at the same time.

We typically only focus on one or a few objects – when this is applied to reading it means that our concentration is focused on a few words only and we pay no attention to anything else until we fix our attention on them. We can broaden the horizontal scope of our eyes when we develop our peripheral vision. This ultimately leads us to recognize more words, resulting in a faster reading speed. We are now going to look at some exercises that will assist in improving peripheral vision.

Thumb Side to Side Exercise

The main aim of this exercise is to stretch the muscles in your eyes to increase their capacity and enable you to read more words.

- Sit or stand up straight and focus your vision straight ahead of you.
- Hold up both of your thumbs at the same time as you slowly stretch your arms out to the sides. Once your arms are level your shoulders, stop stretching.
- While you are still in this position take a look at either one of your arms and see if you can see your thumbs. Don't turn your head when you are doing this, and don't worry if you are unable to see your thumbs. You will get better with practise.
- Glance at each side and try and look at your thumbs 12 times in reps of three.

Recognition Stimulus Exercise

This exercise is going to require you to have a partner and a few materials. The aim of the exercise is to train your eyes to enable them to quickly move from the left to the right. This is the same motion used by the eyes when reading.

- Ask your partner to grab hold of a stimulus object which will be something like a card with a word, color or number on it.
- Get your partner to position themselves on either your left or your right side, keeping an arm's length from you.
- Once they have taken this position, they need to show you the card. You need to

recognize what is shown on the card. Your partner will record your progress and then move to the other side of you and repeat the process, using a different stimulus object.

Eye Writing Exercise

The main aim of this exercise is to give your eyes further and wider vision. It also stretches the muscles in your eyes because of the distance that you are looking.

1. Focus on a wall that is positioned far away from you.
2. Imagine that you are writing your name on the wall with your eyes. Use the same movements with your eyes that you would with your hands.

The Yoga Pose

This is another exercise that will assist in developing your peripheral vision. It involves you keeping a yoga pose at the same time as stretching your eye muscles from left to right. Not only does this exercise help improve your eye muscles, it also helps you to re-focus your brain and wake you up if you are feeling tired.

1. To make sure that you don't lose your balance and fall, stand next to something that you will be able to hold onto. A firm

chair or table will do, but it's not a good idea to stand close to a wall.

2. Stand straight so that your feet are aligned with your shoulders.

3. Keep your head straight and focus on an object that is approximately 10 feet away from your nose.

4. Put your palms together in a praying position and rest them on the front of your chest.

5. At the same time, raise one of your feet so that it is level with your knees.

6. With your head straight, look as far in front of you as you can. Keep your focus on the furthest object that you can see for approximately 30 seconds and then change the leg that you are balancing on. Keep your head in one position. Do three sets of this pose.

Distance Transformation Exercise

Apart from improving the flexibility of your eye muscles and seeing more when they are being stretched in far directions, you also need to work on the ciliary muscle. This is the muscle that is responsible for our lens and it constricts and expands depending upon how far away the object is. This is critical for peripheral vision because if your eyes struggle to see an object from a far distance, it will be more difficult to keep your focus on more than one word. This exercise will help to train your ciliary muscles, which will improve your eyesight.

1. Hold either your finger or a small object a minimum of 6 inches away from the end of your nose. Keep your focus on the object for approximately 10 seconds, or until you are able to see it clearly.
2. When your focus on the object is clear, you will then need to slowly take your attention off it and focus on another object that is located at least 10 feet in front of you. Focus on the object until you are able to see it clearly.
3. Shift your focus back to the closer object and repeat this process 10 times.

You will know when you are doing the exercise correctly because everything else in your vision, apart from the object you are focusing on will become blurry. This exercise is typically recommended for readers who are over the age of 40. Research has shown that it is around this age that the ciliary muscles begin to deteriorate.

Another way of performing this exercise is to take a 10 second break after you have read for 10 full minutes and then focus on an object that is 10 feet away until you are able to see it clearly. Begin reading again, and repeat the exercise after you have read for another 10 minutes.

Computer-aided all direction

eye exercise

The main purpose of this exercise is to assist in improving your eye muscles so that they can move easily in any direction. Despite the fact that the motion the eye uses when reading is horizontal you will find that this exercise becomes even more beneficial when the speed reading finger motion exercise is being used. (This will be introduced in a later chapter).

1. You will need a computer program such as PowerPoint; you will also need to make sure that it has an animation feature such as blink.
2. Type 4 different symbols, numbers or letters on all sides of the page.
3. Apply the blinking animation to the page. Make sure that the blinking timeline is for two numbers at a time and that the symbols change after a certain period of time.

Here is an example: You have written the numbers 3 and 4 on the upper right and left hand corners of the page. On the lower right and left corners, you have written the numbers 5 and 6. You will then need to make them blink in pairs. The numbers 3 and 4 should blink one after another; you should not be able to see the numbers 5 and 6. Repeat the process horizontally and diagonally with either of the two numbers.

4. The next step is to look at the text that has been animated and make sure that your

eyes are following the same movement that is made by the animation effect.

Visual Series Rapid Presentation

This exercise began as an experiment to increase attention span. However, it can also improve reading speed. The pioneers of the idea believed that if a person was capable of reducing their "intentional blink," it enabled them to notice more things, similar to expanding scope of vision. The main aim of this exercise is to train people to be able to focus for a longer period of time without breaking their attention for even a second. When attention has been enhanced, you will be able to speed read at a faster pace

You will need to use a computer for this exercise. You will then be asked to point out the letters or numbers that are being formed while the message is blinking. Here is an example.

You will be asked to find the numbers **9, 1** and **6** hidden within the sequence **eR691N**. Each character is going to be flashed one at a time, but the interval between each flash will be very short. Once the characters have finished flashing, you will then need to locate the position of the stimulus within the sequence. There will only be a few milliseconds for each interval before the next character is shown. This makes it very difficult to recognize, and the entire sequence is only shown for less than a second.

Chunk Reading

You can also strengthen your eyes by using a method referred to as chunk reading. This is where you learn how to read groups of words together. The typical pattern of reading practiced by the majority of people pays attention to one word at a time. Not only does chunking save time when reading; it also helps you to understand the text better because a group of words is easier to understand than one word.

As you practice this method you will become even more familiar with groups of words that are typically used in a sentence meaning that you will be able to quickly move onto the next group of words.

- Select reading material that you find interesting. It doesn't have to be a long text: a short magazine article will be ok. Make sure when you start reading you focus your attention on two words and not just one.

- While you are reading, use a pointer. This will provide you with guidance while you are reading. The pointer should be on the second word if you are reading more than two words at a time. You can either use a pen or your fingers to point at a word. If you are using a reading device such as a tablet or a computer, you can use the mouse.

- Instead of reading from the beginning of the sentence, start reading from the middle. The main aim of this technique is to train the eyes to develop your peripheral vision because you will learn how to read words after and before the phrase. This typically takes place after you are capable of reading three words at a time.

- You should limit your practice to 15 minutes, three times per day. Chunk reading requires that you pay very close attention because you are making a conscious effort to break the old habit of reading one word at a time. This can be very exhausting and your brain will get tired, meaning that once you start to speed read, your reading speed will be affected.

Chunk Reading Exercise

Apart from the guidelines that you are going to have to follow in order to learn this skill, you can also practice the following exercises which will improve your learning speed.

You will need to use your computer to arrange reading material into word groups. If you are reading from your computer, you can learn to chunk read faster by arranging the text into word groups that are meaningful. This is similar to a haiku poem, which has a set number of words. You can customize and edit the material using the office application and you will base this according to the number of words that you wish to use in a group. Here is an example:

When you **are** arranging

The **material** you are going to read into

Word groups **that** are meaningful

 This is what it will look

Like when you have **finished**.

This is the reason why it is easy to read a poem regardless of the length.

Middle words underlined

Apart from arranging the text into word groups that are meaningful you can also use peripheral vision skill to begin reading in the middle of the word group.

In the example that has been presented, observe that some of the words have been underlined. This is the guide that you will use so that your gaze is focused on the word in the middle. After some time, you will extend your peripheral vision so that you can read words on both sides of the underlined word. Due to the fact that the words are formatted differently, your eyes will quickly notice the words that have been underlined and you will then be able to focus on reading those words first. You can use this method to start practising on the middle section of the word group. As these skills are developed, it will improve your ability to read in chunks without having to arrange or format the information.

These methods are useful for developing your reading scope. The peripheral vision exercise will enable you to see the words clearly on the periphery and train your eyes so that you can quickly move them from one side to the next.

Treating Your Eyes and Preventing and Curing Eyestrain

Speed reading puts a considerable amount of strain on your eyes and they need to rest. The more relaxed your eyes are the easier it will be for you to read. Here are some simple tips to prevent and cure eye strain:

- This method is referred to as 'palming'. Get your hands warm by rubbing them together. Close your eyes and use your hands to cover them so that you are unable to see any light. Try not to press on your eyeballs; doing so can cause damage. Leave your hands over your eyes for as long as you can.

- The majority of people who suffer from eye problems make them worse by not blinking. When you don't blink, your eyes dry up. When you are reading, especially if you are doing so on a monitor like a computer, laptop, or iPad, make sure that you blink regularly so you can water your eyes. You might want to put a sign on your monitor reminding you to blink.

- If your eyes feel tired, an eyewash from a local pharmacy should do the trick.

Carefully follow the instructions when you use it, and if you feel that you need to book an appointment with your doctor or your optician do so. Wearing contact lenses makes it even more important to take care of your eyes while reading.

Limit Eye Strain When Reading From a PC

- **Type and Font Size:** If you have been sent a document and either the font size or the type is difficult to read, change them. Serif fonts are quicker and easier to read.

- **Screen Contrast:** Keep your screen clutter free and make sure that the background is has a contrast to the text you are reading.

- **Screen Savers:** You can now get screen savers that are constantly active. These screens will help to relax your eyes.

- **Screen Positions:** The screen should be kept at a comfortable distance away from you. It should be a minimum of an arm's length away. You should also avoid having the screen in front of a window because the light contrasts can be uncomfortable.

- **Comfort:** When you are working at a PC, your fingers are the only parts of your body that get any exercise. Take a break, do some eye exercises and stretch every 20 to 30 minutes.

Chapter 5
Stop Reading Out Aloud

In the last few chapters you have been preparing yourself to begin your speed reading journey. You are now going to learn what NOT to do when you are speed reading.

Sub-Vocalization

This is basically the process of reading out loud, whether you actually vocalize whisper or read it in your mind. There are several reasons as to why the majority of people have developed this habit:

- We have been taught to believe that the only way to avoid reading material more than once is to focus on every word in the text. This process is supposed to enable the reader to work out what the word means right there and then. This results in slow progress in reading and is the same belief held that reading slowly helps the reader to better comprehend the information.

- The majority of people believe that each individual word is what is important in the text. This is factually incorrect. What is important is the meaning of each word combination. It makes it very difficult to work out what the main idea in the text is if you are too focused on the meaning of each individual word before putting them together to form the sentence.

- When children are taught to read, they are taught to read each word out loud. This is the easiest way of developing a child's speech and word pronunciation.

How to Solve the Problem of Sub-Vocalization

It can be difficult to solve the problem of sub-vocalization because the majority of people have been trained to read this way and they are fully capable of understanding the material even if they are not able to speed read. If you want to develop your speed reading ability, you are going to have to stop this habit. Here are some tips to assist you in reversing sub-vocalization:

- Challenge yourself whilst you are reading by timing yourself, and record the number of words you are able to read during a certain time frame. You can keep doing this until you beat your own time. This will enhance your ability to understand the meaning of groups of words as opposed to single words.
- Say a different phrase or word apart from the one you are reading. This process will distract your mind from reading word for word out loud. You can also do this in silence and say other words in your mind other than the material that you are reading. You will find that your eyes are capable of recognizing and understanding

the meaning of words on a page even when you are not reading them out loud. You can also count from 1 to 100 when you are reading as a way of distracting your brain from reading out loud.

- Think about and visualize the word instead of pronouncing it in your head. In order to read, you have to think. This is what makes it possible for you to understand the words you are reading. Instead of thinking how you are going to pronounce the word or phrase, visualize it instead. It won't help to just tell your mind to stop sub-vocalizing because then it becomes even more conscious of the fact that it is sub vocalizing. The best way to combat this habit is to use these methods.

- If you mime your words when you are reading, you will need to keep your mouth busy by chewing gum to prevent you from moving your mouth to say the words.

- The majority of people who sub-vocalize do so because they have a limited vocabulary. They find it difficult to understand the words that have been written in the text. This is especially true if you are encountering the word for the first time. Another method to stop you from sub-vocalizing is to develop an extensive vocabulary. You can enhance your vocabulary by reading the dictionary and other reading materials where you can learn new words which will help you to develop your vocabulary. This means that when you see these words when you are speed reading you will understand them immediately and you won't have to read the word out loud to try and work out what it means. Pre-reading is another helpful tool to assist you in developing your vocabulary because you can get familiar with the words before you start to speed read.

- Learn to focus on the words that are important. This will provide you with an idea of what the sentence is about and limit you to only pronouncing those words. For example, if you are reading the following sentence: "Sarah is working at a hospital so that she can pay for her school fees." You will read each word but the only words you will pronounce are Sarah, hospital, pay, school fees. These words are enough to increase your comprehension and assist you in the remembering the meaning of the words. It will also reduce the number of words that you say in your head.

- When you are reading, ask questions while forming a visual picture of what you are reading in your mind. You will increase your comprehension by asking questions that are directly related to the material you are reading. When you do this, your mind becomes even more active because you are searching for the answers to your questions. This practise will reduce your desire to pronounce each word because your mind will be otherwise engaged in visualizing and searching for answers.

You will not be able to stop sub-vocalizing completely. There are going to be times when it is necessary to read the words out loud. However, it is a proven fact that reading each word out loud limits your ability to understand the text.

Chapter 6
Using Hand Motions to Limit Regressions

Reading material more than once also limits your ability to speed read. This process is referred to as regression. There are several reasons as to why this process has been adopted by the majority of readers.

- The reader finds it difficult to understand the material. When we read material that is not familiar to us, we have the natural tendency to re-read what we have just read to try and understand the information. Not only does regression slow down your reading, it also limits the brain's ability to process information at a faster rate.

- Readers often go back over what they have read because they fear they might have missed something or have missed out on important concepts. However, what we fail to understand is that not everything that we are reading is important. There are some passages that are merely an anecdote, or an introduction. The reason why you can't remember what you have just read is because the information isn't important and there is no need to retain it.

How to Reduce Regression

Here are several methods that you can use to reduce regression while you are reading:

- Use an index card or an opaque ruler to cover the information that you have just read.
- Use your finger or a pointer to guide you as you read, because any form of involuntary movement will capture your attention when you are reading. When the pointer is moving, the eyes and the brain are forced to follow it. This then enables the person to read as many ideas and words as possible in a short space of time.

Hand Motions

It is not enough just to use a pointer; it must also be combined with hand motions in order for it to be effective. Here are some directions to follow:

- Every hand motion should begin with a starting position. You will need to start by placing either your right or your left hand on the page. Your palm should be facing downwards and your thumb should be underneath your palm.
- Relax your fingers and hands on the page, your fingers should be slightly spaced out. When you start reading, you should always make sure that your hand looks like this.

Underlining Movement

This is one of the most basic hand movements you are going to learn and it is recommended for those who are just learning to speed read.

- Begin with your hand in the starting position. Then run your hand steadily and smoothly over the material that you are going to read. This process is similar to underlining certain words in each line. Keep your focus on where your finger is pointed.

- When you reach the last word in the line, raise your finger slightly and move it to the next line by moving your hand in a diagonal direction.

- Repeat both steps until you get to the last line on the page.

Once you become acquainted with this hand motion method you can begin to incorporate the other hand motion methods for faster reading.

S-Hand Movement

This is a hand motion that has similarities to the underlining movement with just a few changes. With this hand motion your hand is not lifted when it is moved to the next line. You can either make a tight "S" movement with the aim being to read the words at a faster rate, or you can do a wide "S" movement which works well when previewing the pages contents.

For the tight "S" movement do the following:

- Begin in the starting position and place your hand on the second line of the page.
- Copy the motion of a backwards S beginning from left to right until you reach the end of the line.
- Once you have reached the end of the line, move your hand to the bottom of the third line in the same location as your finger once was (by this time, your finger will need to be on the right side of the page). Continue to run your finger on that line until it gets to the left side of the page.
- Continue until you have get to the end of the page.

To do the wide "S" movement, all you have to do is repeat the same motion but make the motion bigger. You will still need to start on the left side of the page.

When you are using the s hand movement, the brain is forced to recognize a large number of words at the same time as keeping the motion. This is because the hand skips certain lines and teaches you to recognize words vertically and horizontally.

X-Hand Movement

This is another hand movement that copies the motion of writing the letter. You should only practise this hand movement if you have been speed reading for a while. This involves moving your hand in an angular movement and it is typically used to read information that is written in columns such as magazines and newspaper articles.

- Begin with your hand in the starting position; put your hand onto the first word of the page. Then move your index finger in a diagonal motion as you move along to the other side of the page. You should end approximately five lines below the starting point.

- Change your index finger to the middle finger and make an angular movement to get to the second line of the page (should still be on the right side).

- When your finger is on the second line, move it in a diagonal motion to the left side of the page. Transition through five lines.

- When you reach the left side of the page, go back, but this time use your index finger as the pointer when you are moving upwards. Repeat the previous steps until you get to the end of the page.

This hand motion requires you to switch between the middle and the index fingers. Changing fingers reduces the amount of friction experienced if you were only to use one finger. It is also helpful to use this motion if you want to develop diagonal eye movement at the same time as using your peripheral vision. It will teach you how to recognize words in advance, and make sense of everything that you've seen even if the words are not read in the order they were intended to be read in.

Loop Hand Movement

This movement is similar to the X-hand movement but it is slightly different. This is because while they both use diagonal movements, when using curves as opposed to angles, the motion is changes. If you don't want to shift fingers, this is a good method to use. To do the loop hand movement do the following:

- Your middle or index finger should be positioned on the first word on the page.
- Moving to the right side of the page, make a diagonal movement. You should end on the fourth or the fifth word of the starting point.
- Move up to the second line but make a sharp curve going towards the target line instead of an angle. The movement should be the same as making an infinity symbol.
- When you get to the second line on the right side of the page, repeat the same motion at the same time, following the same number of lines when your finger is moved to either side of the page.
- Repeat each step until you have read though the entire page.

L-Hand Movement

When you combine the X-hand motions and the underlining loop you make the L-hand movement. Although it is typically used to read information that is presented in columns, this also works well when previewing information.

- Begin by placing your hand at the starting position on the third line of the left side of the page.

- Move along the line with your finger in the same motion as the underlining movement.

- When you get to the right side of the line, move your finger to the second line after your starting point.

- Move your finger to the left side of the page in a diagonal motion. You should end on the fifth line from where you began.

- When you get to the left side, make a curving motion travelling two lines up from the location where the diagonal movement ended.

- At this point, repeat step two and continue until you have read all of the material on the page.

The underlining motion combined with other motions will enable you to focus on specific lines in the material instead of using just the loop or X hand movements on their own.

Question Mark Movement

If you are planning on previewing the important points in the text, it is recommended that you use the question mark method. This hand motion is a lot quicker in comparison to other hand motions. You can also use this hand motion to train your brain and eyes to recognize more words in a shorter space of time. You will need to follow these steps:

- Place your hand in the starting position. The first word on the page should be your starting point.
- Move your finger in a question mark motion. This motion is similar to the wide S movement.
- Your hand should end at the middle of the last line in the page. Repeat the movement for all the other pages.

Apart from training your eyes to recognize as many words as possible on the page, you will also learn how to read in both directions doing so horizontally. This is due to the fact that the question mark motion requires that you land on the bottom center of the page It is also required that you read the final line of every page so that you will easily be able to follow the contents on the next page.

Chapter 7
Speed Reading Exercises

Before you start speed reading, you will need to consider the following factors that contribute to your ability, or lack of ability to read faster. They are as follows:

Before you Start Speed Reading

- **A Clear Purpose: You** should always know the main purpose for why you are reading something. The clearer your purpose, the quicker you will be able to read through the text and locate it.

- **Mood:** If you are feeling restless, irritable, impatient, or tired you will not be able to read quickly as compared to if you were feeling relaxed, happy, fresh and alert. However, you may not always great when you have to read. Learning how to manage and recognize your feelings so that you will be able to concentrate regardless of how you are feeling is not always going to be easy; however, it is possible.

- **Familiar with the Subject and its Terminology:** If you already have an understanding of the subject, you will have a framework that you can build on. You are more likely to read quickly because you won't have to stop and think about the meaning of certain words.

- **Difficulty of the Text:** Some books are hard to read regardless of whether you are familiar with the subject or not.
- **Stress Levels and Urgency:** Have you noticed that when there is an urgency attached to what you need to read, you find it difficult to read quickly? Speed reading will help you to overcome this problem because it will sharpen your focus and improve your ability to concentrate.

Factors That Affect Your Ability to Speed Read

- A positive attitude towards reading. You should want to improve your reading capability.
- A good vocabulary and familiarity with your subject's terminology.
- A good basic understanding of the subject. If you are learning something new have a strategy in place to build your background knowledge.
- You will need to practice. Setting aside 30 minutes a day for 30 days to speed read will greatly enhance your comprehension, recall and the speed at which you read.

Applying   the   Skills   You

Already Have

You can begin to read more effectively by applying the skills you have already acquired:

- Read a book like a newspaper to get its message.
- Use a book like a dictionary to get specific information.

Don't allow your books to use you; instead, use them. Whether you think that you don't or you think that you do, you already have several reading skills. You already know how to quickly extract information from emails, dictionaries, newspapers etc. Begin to think about how you can use the skills that you already posses when reading books. If you haven't already noticed, you use different methods for reading different materials.

Newspapers

You never sit and read a newspaper word for word; you scan it and look for information that's of interest to you. You look at the headlines and the pictures, and then decide what interests you and read those articles in more detail. You don't pay any attention to information that's irrelevant to you. You stop reading when you have enough information and discard the rest of the newspaper. **Read books like a newspaper to get the main message**.

Dictionaries

When you use any type of reference book, you search for the word or the idea that you need and once you have found it, you close the book. If you are looking for specific information in a book, you don't have to read every page. Use the contents page or the index or flick through the book and look at the chapter headings until you find what you are looking for.

Emails

The majority of people are already competent at sifting through their emails, deleting spam, filing, scanning for necessary information and dealing with things that are quick and urgent.

Factual Books

The speed reading techniques that you are about to learn are specifically designed to help you to extract information that you need from factual books that you don't necessarily want to read for pleasure.

These speed reading techniques can be used with all kinds of reading materials such as journals, eBooks, online reading and reports.

Have a SMART purpose

In business, professionals often set a 'SMART' goal or purpose. You can also apply this technique to reading.

SMART stands for

Specific

Measurable

Achievable
Real
Timed

Analyzing Your Purpose

You have decided to read this book which means you've already set a purpose. Now measure your purpose against the SMART criteria – starting backwards.

Timed: Work with all books in 20 minute sessions. Stick to a time limit of 20 minutes.

Real: Make sure that the reason you have for reading is real; in other words don't make up a reason just for the sake of reading. Read because you actually need to get something from the book. **R** can also stand for **relevant**; ask yourself if the information is relevant to you, and how you are going to use the information.

Achievable: Your purpose has to be realistic and achievable. Having a goal such as wanting to read an entire library in one month isn't going to happen! Also stick to single pieces of information. Trying to search for more than one thing at a time is only going to confuse you.

Measurable: If you can't measure something, it becomes very difficult to know whether or not you have achieved it. For example, you might want to get through four investment techniques in one 20 minute session.

Specific: The more tightly defined and clear your purpose the more information you will be able to extract from the material. Make sure that you know how you are going to use the information because it will make it easier for your brain to locate what you need.

80/20 Rule

The 80/20 rule states that 20% of the effort that you put into anything that you do results in achieving 80% of your goal. Therefore, a low variable percentage within any large system can produce a high percentage. In reading, the idea is that if you are satisfied with achieving 80% of your main purpose, this will result in you gaining five times more information in the same amount of time. It is also believed that more than 80% of the message is found in less than 20% of the words, which is why it is beneficial to search for key information. In practice, 80% of progress is found in 20% of the effort you put in.

The 80/20 rule is also referred to as the Pareto Principle. It was coined by Vilfredo Pareto an Italian economist who noticed that 20% of the peapods in his garden produced 80%of the peas.

Don't Read the Words, Read the Message

It isn't necessary to read each word when you concentrate on the meaning of the message. A small percentage of reading has something to do with how your eyes work; it is mostly to do with the way in which your brain works. It is important that you keep your focus on the message and not on every word that makes up the message.

Typically, it's not required that you read every word in a sentence. Language is very predictable and you can generally guess what's going to come next. Also our brains are wired to decode messages and detect patterns even when there is incomplete information. You can assimilate information faster by focusing on the message and not the words.

Dipping

After you have read quickly to find important information, you can then 'dip' and read the relevant sections more slowly. Once you have got a good understanding of the point, you can speed up again.

Guided Reading

Get a book; any book will do; and a pen. This isn't a writing exercise, so keep the lid on the pen.

Read a portion of the book and use the pen as a pointer. Move the pen along the page at a steady pace, and keep the pen just above or underneath the words that you are reading. This exercise requires that you don't move your eyes backwards, meaning that you are not allowed to go over what you have read again. The pen and your eyes move in one direction only: forwards. Don't worry if you are unable to understand what you are reading. While you are changing your reading habits and practicing, comprehension isn't the point.

As you move through this guided reading exercise you will slowly start to increase the speed that the pen moves. Continue to increase the speed until you can just about understand one or two words on each line. The main aim of this exercise is to train your brain and your eyes to read steadily without backtracking.

Note: Make sure that when you do this exercise, you actually rest the pen and not just point it at the first or last words of every line.

Stretching Comprehension and Speed

This is a short exercise that will increase your reading speed and enhance your memory.

- Use a pacer and read one page as fast as possible.
- Stop and write everything you can remember from what you have just read.
- Every day read five pages and slowly increase the number of pages that you read before stopping to remember what you read.
- Start with a topic that you are familiar with and as you notice an improvement in your speed and comprehension move onto something more challenging.

- The second phase of this exercise requires you to read for 1 minute and then count the number of lines you have read.
- Keep reading for another 1 minute but this time read two extra lines.
- Repeat the exercise for another minute this time reading four more lines. Repeat this until you reach ten lines.
- Always read for recall and good comprehension. If at any point you think that you don't remember or understand the text, consolidate the information and then gradually speed up.

In order to read fast you need to be able to concentrate. If you are finding it difficult to remember or understand what you read it is probably because you are not concentrating properly. As you increase your ability to concentrate, you can increase the time from 2 minutes to 4 minutes etc.

Exercises to Increase Your Flexibility and Your Speed Reading Rate

For the following exercises, you will need to use books that you enjoy reading. Even if the books are not about subjects that you are familiar with, they should be about subjects that you are interested in learning about.

Once you have gotten comfortable with the

exercises, you can start using books with material that is more difficult to comprehend. This could include material that you have to read for study, work or that you are not necessarily interested in. When you are practising with this type of material, make sure that the time limits that you set are strict ones. If not, you will get bored really quickly and want to move onto something that you have more interest in.

Treat these exercises as challenges and games, and spend no more than 10 minutes on each one.

Warm – Up

This is a 5 minute warm up exercise.

- Read for 1 minute with good comprehension.
- Mark the point that you have reached after 1 minute.
- Add half a page to what you have just read and put a mark at that point.
- Go back to the beginning and read for one minute with good comprehension until you get to the second mark for 1 minute.
- When you are comfortable with reaching the mark at the second point add another half a page and mark that spot.
- Go back to the beginning and read with good comprehension for 1 minute until you get to the third mark.
- Continue with this process until you have reached the fifth mark.

- By this time, you will probably realize that you are not actually reading and this is the whole point of the exercise. The aim is that you see each word just enough to recognize that it is an English word. This will help you to get used to recognizing/seeing more than one word at a time.

Increase Your Speed Flexibility

- Choose a text on a subject that you are familiar with.
- Begin by reading slowly almost word for word.
- Speed up as you finish the first paragraph. Speed up your rate of reading until you are reading as fast as you can but can still understand the text.
- When you start reading faster than you are comprehending, you will need to slow down.
- You will now start to practice flexible reading.
- Read the first sentence of the paragraph quite slowly and then speed up as you move through the paragraph and slow down when you arrive at sections that you don't understand.
- When you have been reading a book on a subject that you are familiar with for some time, switch to a book with a subject that

you are not familiar with and start the exercise again.

- Now compare both experiences. What did you find? Did you notice that it was easier to read the familiar book?

Novel Exercise

Novels are good practice materials to enhance your flexibility in pacing. At the beginning of the novel you might find that you are pacing under every line. When the story begins to accelerate and you are searching for the exciting parts between the descriptions, you may find that you move the pacer down the middle of the page until you come to the parts of the story that really make the novel. You won't enjoy the novels any less and you will actually find that you are able to finish more novels then you did previously.

Metronome Pacing

If you don't have one already, buy a small electronic metronome that has an audible tick but isn't too loud.

Work on this exercise for 2 minutes and then have a 5 minute break.

- Set the metronome at its slowest pace and read one line for each tick.
- Every half a page or every page, increase the metronome pace by one tick. If you are comfortable with this pace, you can increase it by more.

- Take a break and then keep going. Repeat the exercise until you have reached the fast speed.

The metronome will get to a speed where it's impossible for you to read every word. This exercise forces your brain and eyes to absorb and see more than one word at a time, and gradually increases your ability.

Food for Thought

As you are driving on a freeway at 75 mph, you get off an exit and arrive at a town where you suddenly have to reduce your speed to 30mph. You might think that's the speed you are travelling at until you are stopped by the police who inform you that you are travelling at 40 mph when you thought that you had slowed down to 30 mph. The similarity between speed reading and driving doesn't end there. When you are driving at 90mph, it is essential that you are concentrating and you can't afford to admire the scenery. When you are speed reading, your mind doesn't have the desire to wander as much as it would want to at '30 mph.'

Super-Duper Reading

Look down the middle of the page quickly (1-4 seconds). Allow your finger to guide you for around 10 pages or until you start making sense of some of the words. Then keep reading with comprehension. Notice the difference as you read at an increased speed because your brain is now used to reacting faster.

How to Super-Duper Read

- Inhale deeply. As you exhale smile and keep your focus.
- Position your finger underneath the center word on the top line of the page or the column.
- Keep your focus on the words that are just above your finger.
- Run your finger down the page smoothly and keep your eyes focused on the word above it. You should spend around four seconds on each page.
- You will start to notice words after page 6 or 7. When you start noticing words, start reading normally but at a faster speed.
- Go back to the start of the section and read it again as quickly as you have the ability to comprehend the information.

Skittering

The purpose of skittering is to allow your eyes to jump around the page so that you can focus on the hot spots of the text, or on words that appear to give you the main idea of the nature of the text. There are two ways that you can skitter:

1. Randomly – Allow your eyes to glance over different areas on the page.

2. Any Pattern – Choose a pattern in which to read, this can either be a zigzag, a diagonal or a question, whichever you are most comfortable with.

A zigzag is a common pattern for skittering, depending on the density of the information the pattern is either tight or loose.

Capital I Shape

1. Read the first three lines of the page.
2. Super read through the middle of the page.
3. Read the final three lines.

The majority of people find that this technique is the first step on their speed reading journey.

First and Last

Read the first few lines and the last few lines on a page. In a text that is densely written you will need to read the first and the last lines of each section or paragraph in order to get a better understanding of the contents.

When you do this if you find that the key points are not located in the beginning or ending of the paragraphs or sections, you only need to read the middle section of the text. When the first and last pattern is applied to the entire book, it is referred to as beginning and ending.

Often times it will be enough to read only the first couple of lines on every page. You should try and read an entire book using this method.

—

Remember by Doing

If you want to remember the information that you are reading, you will need to take the necessary steps to improve your memory. This includes active reading at the same time as taking notes, discuss it with someone and review it.

If you are an expert in a certain subject, you will probably remember any new information that's related to your subject easily. This is because you are already very familiar with the subject and your brain will have several hooks in which to attach the new information.

If you are new to the subject, or if you are studying something that you are not particularly interested in, you will have to make a conscious effort to remember the new information that you are learning.

How to Remember Information

The purpose of speed reading techniques is to assist you in taking in information and retaining it. You should also take note of the following:

- Only remember what is necessary. Before you start to use memory techniques you will have to decide which information is worth remembering. If you try and remember everything you will fail. That is definitely a recipe for disaster.

- Read with a questioning and active mind. Think about, summarize and articulate the key messages. Arrange the ideas in order of importance. Ask yourself whether you agree. What's new? What information is missing?

- You will need to repeat all the information that you want to remember. Your memory processes and retains through repetition.
- Make written and mental associations and links between what you already know and any new ideas. The more ideas you have linked together the better.
- To connect the facts it is advised that you make up stories. Use exaggeration, colors, and images. It could be a strong emotion or something funny. Visualize exceptional things because they are what will stand out in your memory.
- Taking naps and sleeping helps with memory consolidation.

Take Notes with Rhizomaps and Mind maps

The first step to retaining information is to take notes. Rhizomaps and mind maps are easier to remember and they lead to great creativity when using linear notes. If you are not at your desk, you will need to write on post-it notes and stick them to your book.

I suggest that you take notes in one of two ways:

1. Rhizomapping: Developed by Susan Norman and Jan Cisek
2. Mind mapping: Developed by Tony Buzan

- Note-making is the process of generating your own ideas.
- Note-taking is the process of taking ideas from other sources such as lectures or books. You can use both rhizomaps and mind maps for this.

Mind mapping

A mind map begins with a keyword or a picture in the center position, as a representation of the topic. Several branches protrude from the key word. On every branch there is a short phrase or a word that demonstrates how the key idea is related. Smaller branches are used to summarize secondary ideas. Smaller branches are used to summarize examples. You can use pictures or color to make your mind map even easier to remember.

The key to creating a good mind map is to get your ideas together in a clear and concise way using a minimum number of words, and then use the twigs and the branches to demonstrate the relationship between the ideas.

When Mind mapping is Helpful: You should use mind mapping when you want to show that there is a connection between ideas. Use a mind map to do the following:

- Set up a structure for syntopic processing or a 20 minutes work session.
- To make it clear that you already know certain information about a subject and to

identify whether or not there are any gaps in your knowledge. You should do this before you start reading so that you can add to the mind map.

- Anytime you are note-taking and you are already familiar with the structure of the subject and how everything works together.
- For step by step sequential notes.
- When you have some random notes and you want to organize your ideas (or from a rhizomap) to enable you to present them during a presentation, to write an essay or a report.

Rhizomapping

A rhizomap involves jotting down random ideas on a piece of paper. As you come across more ideas that connect with what you have already written, you write those ideas next to it. If you need to you can reorganize the ideas once you have completed the map by highlighting the most important ideas. You can also link the ideas by using underlining, arrows, stars, color-coding and numbering.

When Rhizomapping is Helpful: It is a good idea to use rhizomapping when you are not sure of the structure of the subject that you are going to be reading about. For example, you are trying to understand the overview of a subject that's completely new to you. Or when you are uncertain of what type of useful information you are going to get from a book. You can also use a rhizomaps to present information.

Write in Your Books

If you are reading while you are on public transport and are unable to draw a mind map or a rhizomap, you will need to keep yourself engaged in the reading process by underlining or highlighting key ideas in your reading material. You can also record your notes on a post it note and stick it in the book. If you want to make those notes more permanent, you can do so by creating a rhizomap or a mind map later on. This will help you to remember them more effectively. When you are reading an EBook, you can do the same by making notes, adding bookmarks, and searching through the content. You can also see what other people have underlined, which will enable you to take advantage of crowd wisdom by focusing on the areas of the book that have been highlighted the most.

Twenty Minute Sessions

A work out session involves combining all of the speed reading techniques together and using them to get the information that you need. Have a work out session for twenty minutes with one clear purpose and one book. If you still feel as if you need to get more out of a book, you should have a break and then go back to it. Each time you work out with one book should be limited to twenty minutes.

How to Have a Workout Session

- Before you start your workout session, make sure that you preview the book to make sure it has all the information that you need.
- What is your main purpose for this? Are you looking to get an idea of the message or are you looking for specific information?
- Sit comfortable at a table and make sure you have good light and anything else that you might need.
- Get into a good, relaxed but alert mental state and keep a questioning mind.
- Set your alarm for 20 minutes making sure the time source is in full view.
- Start searching through the book to find the information you need to fulfil your purpose. You can use the index and the speed-reading patterns to search for information hot spots.
- Use rhizomaps and mind maps to take notes as you go along.
- Make sure you keep looking at the time and you have a clear purpose in mind. Don't be tempted to slow down and read for leisure. Keep searching for the information that will fulfil your purpose.
- When the 20 minutes is up, make sure you stop.

- Check how much of your purpose you have achieved and think about how long it would have taken you to get to this level of understanding using traditional reading methods.
- If there is anyone around, take five minutes to talk to them about the information you have discovered.
- Review how much of your purpose has been achieved. Discussing it will give you a fair idea of what you have achieved. If you have managed to achieve 80% of your purpose, you can then congratulate yourself for succeeding with the 80/20 rule. If you have achieved less, you will need to decide how much longer you need to achieve your goal.
- Think about what you have learned from the experience and consider what you can do the next time to improve.
- Take a 10 minute break.
- When your break is over, think about what else you need, including the following:

  - A few more minutes to fully achieve your purpose.
  - Make a plan for another workout session.
  - Do a rapid read over from front to back so you can get more information.

- Celebrate your success because you have already achieved your purpose.

Discuss What you Need

When you talk about what you need to do, it helps you make your ideas clear in your mind and helps you remember them. Do the following twice:

1. Summarize the information to yourself as you are reading. This will keep you actively engaged.
2. When you have finished reading, tell someone about what you have read. This helps you to memorize and understand the information better.

Regularly Review Information

In general, people forget 90% of what they read within 48 hours of reading the information. By spending a couple of minutes reviewing your notes the following day, a week and a month later you will remember between 80 and 90% of the information!

Due to the fact that repetition is the key to remembering, you will need to continuously review the information that you have studied. If not, it is completely normal for the brain to forget. You only need to spend a few minutes with each review. You should review your notes

after the following time periods:
- 1 day
- 1 week
- 1 month

When you are reviewing information, make sure you record it in note form. You should then go back and compare it with what was previously written. Go back to the original text to check any details you are uncertain of. By using this method to test your memory you will greatly improve your ability to memorize information. Research has confirmed that the only way to build recall is to practise it.

When you review information you are capable of remembering almost 100% of what you originally read. After some experience, it becomes much easier to remember information this way.

Using Different Speeds to Read Texts

The majority of people read everything at the same pace and that is a slow one. There is nothing wrong with slow reading in certain circumstances such as correcting and proof reading, if you are having fun reading slowly or if you like the sound of the words. However, when you want to get information out of the text it is a good idea to use speed reading techniques.

Not only does speed reading help you read more quickly, it also provides you with choices about how you choose to read different materials.

Syntopic Processing

Syntopic processing involves reading four books at the same time instead of one. You will have a 75 minute session spending around 15 minutes on each book, and you will gather and compare information with the purpose of fulfilling one goal. Take a few minutes break in between books. At the end you will evaluate the information using a rhizomap or a mind map.

You can work with a minimum of two books when you are using this technique, but ideally you should use four. All books should be on the same subject, and your purpose will need to be the same. Use the same method to read each book as when you do a 20 minute work-out session.

If you are not sure of what your goal should be, here are some ideas:

- Finding information to answer an essay question
- Finding information to write a report or an article
- Finding information for a talk or a presentation
- Creating an overview for a new subject
- Making a decision after you have overviewed all of the factors you need to consider

- Locating specific techniques you can use while you are at work so that you can achieve a particular outcome.

How to use Synoptic Processing

- The first step will be to state your purpose, making sure that it is specific, contextualised, and clear.
- You will then need to preview any books that are relevant to your purpose; you should take about three minutes for each book. Choose the best books to help you achieve your purpose.
- Prepare the structure of your rhizomap or your mind map by thinking about the questions that you want to answer and how you plan on displaying your notes.
- Decide on a time frame for all four books reading each in 15 minute intervals and taking 15 minutes for a break. Set your timer for the first 15 minute session.
- Get into a receptive mental state.
- Find key information in the first book and then record it on one of your maps. After each 15 minutes is over move onto a new book.
- When you are half way through, take a short break so you can stretch and get back into the right frame of mind.
- At the end of each session, take a few minutes to go over your work and to look

over the books where you found the most information.

- Once you have completed the task, analyze how much of your purpose you have achieved. You can then celebrate your success.
- Discuss what you have learned with someone else.

Tips

- A timer will help you to keep track of the time.
- Quickly move onto another book if you find that the book doesn't contain the information that you need.
- Make sure that you move onto the next book at the next session; don't be tempted to keep going over the material you have already read.
- Don't go over the 15 minute time frame. You can do anything extra at the end of the session if you need to.

Sharpen Your Focus by Adding a Joker

As well as your four books, you should also add a joker book. This is a randomly chosen short book that has no relevance to the subject. It will help you to think more creatively and actively about your subject. When you have completed the first book, you should spend five minutes on the joker book. Have a look through it and think about how it could make you think differently about your subject and purpose. It may even give you some content. It might help you to see the bigger picture, take a different approach to the task, or present the information in a more imaginative way.

Your Synopic Processing Should Include the Following:

- Decide on your purpose
- Find your books and preview them
- Gather all the things that you are going to need for the session.

[09:59] Get yourself into a good state (1 minute)
[10:00] Get started with the first book and make notes as you read (15 minutes)
[10:15] Read your joker book to get a different point of view (5 minutes)
[10:20] Move onto the second book (15 minutes)
[10:35] Take a break for 2 minutes and stretch
[10:37] Move onto the third book (15 minutes)
[10:52] Move onto the fourth book (15 minutes)
[11:07] Review all the books for 7 minutes or go over your notes and get them into order.
[11:14] Stop

- Go over how much of your purpose you have achieved.
- Discuss what you have learned with someone.
- Think about what you have learned from the experience and decide what you

would do differently if you were to do it again.
- Celebrate your success

Stick to the Timeframes You Have Set

When you have given yourself a certain timeframe in which to do something it encourages you to work quickly and focus on your purpose. It also encourages you to continue on with future work out sessions.

Once you have become familiar with a few of the speed reading techniques you will find that you will start instinctively judging how long any given material will take you to read and gather the information that you need. However, when you have just started and you are trying to get rid of old habits it is a good idea to set yourself a time frame. It will benefit you greatly to invest in a timer.

Time Recommendations
- No more than 5 minutes for previewing
- No more than 20 minutes for each book
- No more than 75 minutes for synoptic processing using four books and a joker

Cover to Cover Rapid Read

After a work session, go through each page of the book for approximately 2 to 10 seconds per page.

Search for key information.

Reading from the beginning to the end of a book means that you quickly go through a book in sequence, looking for key information.

Rapid Reading Technique

Look through the book quickly; you will need to spend 2-10 seconds on every page. Use your favorite speed reading patterns to search for hotspots. When you have found your hotspots you can reduce your reading speed (dip) and read around the information until you have fully understood the point that is being made. Start rapid reading again and take notes.

Why Read From Front to Back

- Speed readers who are less experienced generally rapid read after they have had a 20 minute workout session. They use this technique to check for any information they have missed. Due to the fact that you have become acquainted with the book when previewed it and because of the work session, it becomes very easy to locate key information. Rapid reading can be a great help when you have just started speed reading because it helps you to overcome the feeling that you will miss information if you don't read the material from front to back. As you become more experienced with your speed reading capabilities, the 80/20 rule and your ability to quickly gather information, you will no longer need to use the rapid reading technique and you can spend that time reading other material.

- Experienced speed readers generally rapid read a book as opposed to doing a work session, when their main aim is to get an overview of the material and or to get a message.

Get the Overview Before You Get the Details

When you have just started to learn a new subject, make sure that you understand the bigger picture, and that you understand the overview before you start to look at the details. Due to the fact that the majority of books are written in sequence this means that you can preview and look at chapter and section headings and then the first and the last chapters for a general understanding. Synoptic processing is a great way of getting an overview for a new subject.

This is the best technique for finding a good purpose and can make the difference between success and failure when you are trying to use other techniques. Anytime you learn something new, the brain learns best by getting an overview of the subject before going into further detail.

How to Create an Overview

When you are learning about a new subject and you don't have any knowledge about it at all, there are several ways that you can create an overview.

- Conduct an internet search by typing in the subject line and reading the definitions or the introductory articles.
- Ask an expert mentor for guidance.
- Read a children's book on the same subject.
- Go through the first year college course bookish on the subject and then preview all the books on the list for 3 to 5 minutes per day.
- Go to a bookshop or a library and preview the introductory books on the subject that you are studying and then select the ones that you think are going to be the most useful.
- If you have a few books on the subject, draw a rhizomap or a mind map for the overview of the subject.

Your main purpose should be to record all of the key areas in your subject (the chapter headings in each book will usually work) you should have a basic idea of what each area is referring to. (Spend the majority of your time making sure that you understand what is written in the contents). When you understand the big picture, you will have a much better idea of the overall picture. At this point you will be able to go into as much detail as you wish in any of the areas, having full confidence that you know how they are interrelate to other areas of the subject.

There will be times when the details are not important. In such instances, the bigger picture is going to be just enough. But even if you do require all of the details, it is easier for them to be fitted into a pattern than to get them sequentially and separately.

Reading Summaries

The quickest way to get the message of a book is to read the summary. Research has found that people remember more information and for a longer period of time when they read summaries as opposed to reading the entire book. You should always check whether a book contains chapter summaries because reading all of these will quickly give you an overview of what the book is about.

While you are reading, search for phrases that indicate whether or not the author is providing a summary. These will include words such as "in a nutshell," "in summary," or "to sum up."

It will be even better if you find a summary of the entire book or several published compilations of summaries. You will also find that a good review of the book will provide you with a summary or the key message.

As you are reading the summary, make sure that you are taking notes using a mind map or a rhizomap.

Download the Book

No, I don't mean download the book onto your

computer. The book should be downloaded into your subconscious mind. You can do this by quickly looking at each double page without making a conscious effort to understand or to see the text. Simply trust that the information has been downloaded into your subconscious mind. Once you have done this, incorporate your preferred speed reading techniques and you will begin to realize that you are learning more and more information because what has been downloaded in your subconscious starts to become a part of your conscious awareness.

This is the most difficult technique to understand but it is the easiest technique to implement. It is different from the other strategies and techniques because you are relying on your subconscious mind. You are not required to read anything consciously. The main aim of downloading is to expose your subconscious mind to the contents of the book so that it can be transferred into your long-term memory.

The Downloading Process

- Hold the book in a way that you can easily see all four corners of the book when it is open.
- Relax and smile. The more you enjoy this process the easier it will be.
- Begin to turn the pages, one at a time, and do so quickly making sure that you can see the four corners of the book in your peripheral vision. Don't make any attempt

to read the information. Just make sure that the words are positioned before your eyes.

- If your hand starts to get tired, you can turn the book upside down and use your other hand. It doesn't matter which way the book is turned your brain will still be able to interpret the words.
- When you have reached the end of the book, flick through the book forwards and backwards as you look at it.
- Work on something else for another 20 minutes. Taking a nap if you can is ideal. You need to do this in order for the brain to organize the information that it has downloaded.

That's the end of the process. You will definitely feel as if you haven't understood a word of what you've looked at because consciously you haven't. However, unconsciously you have transferred all of the information into your long term memory.

Please Note:
- It doesn't matter whether the words are blurred or clear.
- Concentration isn't required.
- Make sure that the information that is downloaded means something to you.

When to Download

—

You can use the downloading technique at any time; however, we recommend that you use it for the following:

- Once you have determined what your purpose is.
- After you have worked with a book.
- When you need to gather some information in advance (a minimum of 24 hours).
- Just before you go to bed because the brain processes its information best when you are sleeping.
- Only when the information is required.

The best way to transfer the downloaded information to your conscious mind is to continue to use the speed reading techniques. Repetition sends a message to the unconscious mind that this is something that you are interested in, and stimulates the conscious mind to receive it.

Downloading for Direct Learning

Download a number of different books which contain strategies for a physical skill that you want to acquire. For example, swimming, or information for a games night. Continue swimming and go to the games night and you will notice a great improvement in your performance. Direct learning means that you download books so that you can learn a skill or results without doing anything to bring this information into your conscious awareness. This technique is solely reliant upon the subconscious mind to recognize the information and transfer it into your subconscious mind.

How to Download for Direct Learning

- Decide what skill you wish to improve and set it as your main purpose. For example: perfecting your golf swing.
- Close your eyes and visualize that you have achieved the results that you want. This exercise helps you to clarify your purpose, and it will help you to recognize when you have achieved it.
- Preview no more than three books that are most likely to teach you the skill that you desire to learn. Make sure that the book provides practical instructions and not theoretical concepts about the skill.
- Go through the download process. You won't feel as if you have learned anything.
- Without thinking about it, put the skill into practice.
- You will start to notice improvements as time goes on.

Read a Book More Than Three Times

Going through a book a number of times using different speed reading techniques will provide you with an increased amount of knowledge concerning the subject.

The majority of people read factual books as if

they are novels; this is generally done in sequence and very slowly. However, it does nothing to help you to remember the information.

- Previewing provides you with an overview.

- A single 20 minute session with a clear purpose provides you with much more information you can use than you would get from traditional reading. If you wish you can do more than one 20 minute session.

- You can also do a cover to cover rapid read or you can download the book. Either method will enable you to take in more information with your subconscious mind.

Even if you combined all three processes, you would still read quicker than in the traditional way and because repetition is one of the keys to retaining information you will be able to remember more information.

Conclusion
Your Journey Has Only Just Began

I'm glad you've made it to the end of the book! I hope that you have been putting the speed reading techniques into practice and that you have already experienced a dramatic improvement in your reading ability. Before you go, take the time to go through some final speed reading tips -- some of them have already been introduced to you, but as you now know, repetition will enhance your ability to memorize.

Put Your Trust in the Process

Trust that the more you use the speed reading techniques the better your skills will become, and the more you will have faith in the process.

The more you use the speed reading techniques you will find that it becomes easier to locate the information that you need. The more you are able to trust in the process, you will lose the fear that you have missed something from not reading the entire book word for word.

The more you work with books; you will start to pick out information more quickly. You will also be confident enough to put the book down without completing it and trust that when you need the information it will be there for you.

Use Different Techniques for Different Materials

Everyone reads different material for different purposes. Try and use different speed reading technique combinations. No one book is the same, and because of this you should use different speed reading techniques with different books according to your main purpose.

Fitting the Pieces Together

Books that contain chapter summaries, subheads, and informative titles make speed reading a lot easier. There are some books that can be a bit more difficult. However, the best advice that I can give you is before you start reading, get into a receptive state. You can also download or rapid read from front to back trusting that the information will be programmed into your subconscious mind.

When a book is written with a lot of examples and stories you can use any of the techniques, especially:

- Note taking
- 20 minute sessions
- Purpose
- Previewing.

Make your main aim to cut through the information and arrive at key ideas. Read a couple of the stories to make the key ideas more memorable and to bring the information to life.

When you are reading a book that has a continuous storyline, such as historical material, a biography, or a novel, read in sequence and also incorporate:

- super-duper reading to speed up your brain
- Rapid reading to quickly look at each page at the same time as using patterns
- Skittering to search for key information hot spots
- Beginnings and endings
- Profitable previewing
- Downloading

We refer to these books as 'train reading' because they are perfect for reading on public transport. As you are reading, make notes or highlight, or write on post-it notes. Later on you can transfer your notes into a mind map, a report or whatever device suits you.

When books are information heavy and dense, for example, manuals and textbooks which provide a lot of summaries and facts, you can use your own examples in order to make the information more memorable and personally relevant. In order to do this you will need to do the following:

- Preview to get an overview of the subject
- Conduct a 20 minute work session with a purpose several times
- Keep changing the focus until you begin to gain more and more knowledge.

Physical Factors

When you are working with a book, make sure that you sit at comfortably at a table, with a pen and paper so that you can take notes. Hold the book at a 45 degree angle so that it is facing towards you, as opposed to the book being flat on the table. Make sure that you are in a receptive mental state.

You Might Also Want to Think About

- **Lighting:** Make sure that you have a good level of ambient lighting as well as direct light. Florescent and natural light is preferred.
- **Breaks:** Take breaks often, stretch, drink water and do some eye exercises.
- **Position:** To find the best reading position you are going to have to experiment.
- **Sleep:** Make sure that you get enough rest during the night. 7-8 hours is a good amount.

Set Your Expectations High

People have a bad habit of reducing their expectations in case of failure. Due to this limited mind-set, the results are even less than expected. If you aim high you will achieve more. Increase your expectations by striving for more, and setting tighter time limits. You will soon start to see results that exceed your expectations.

As you implement the techniques in this book, make sure that you set high expectations about what you are capable of achieving in a short amount of time. As you start to increase your speed set higher goals for yourself.

Develop Good Habits

When you are in the beginning stages of learning a new skill it takes a substantial amount of effort. Once you have put in that effort, you don't need to keep putting in more effort; your job is to sustain it. Your new skill will gradually become a habit and you won't need to put in as much effort.

Ironically, people typically give up just as things are about to start getting easier. The thought process is that it's not worth putting in all the effort and so they stop. All that is required when putting a new skill into practice is to maintain your determination, followed by patience, and persistence and eventually you will notice you are capable of doing it without putting in any effort at all.

Celebrate Success

Your brain is wired to pay attention to your mistakes and failure. However, you can train yourself to notice when you succeed which will encourage future success.

Read More

If you read more, especially when you are using

the speed reading techniques, you will become a better reader. The more you read, the more you will expand your vocabulary and the easier it will be for you to read.

Beginning and Ending

You will often find key information at the beginning and ending of the books or chapters, so this is the first place that you should look.

Look at the Chapter

There are two types of first chapters or introductions. One of them is very helpful and will get your attention by telling you what the book is about and the direction that it's heading. It's basically providing you with an overview of the subject. This is the chapter that you should read first.

The second type of first chapter is not so great. It's the type that provides you with a lot of tedious unnecessary details that don't provide you with any incentive to keep reading. You can skip this chapter and move onto the second method to beginnings.

The Second Method to Beginnings

Read a few lines of the first paragraph of each chapter. This will provide you with an overview of what the book is about. Then read the first few lines of each page of the book. This can be enough to provide you with an understanding of the main message of the book. You can also use it as a way to locate hotspots of information which could lead you to look at the page for extra details.

Read the End First

The majority of people naturally turn to the end of a book before they start reading from the beginning. This is a very effective reading technique. Try reading the final chapter of a book first because it generally summarizes the main points that the author is trying to make. You will then only need to skim through the book to look for explanations of the things that you don't understand. You should also search for summaries at the end of chapters.

THE END............
            I wish you continued success on your speed reading journey!

FREE DOWNLOAD

INSIGHTFUL GROWTH STRATEGIES FOR YOUR PERSONAL AND PROFESSIONAL SUCCESS!

My friends and colleagues Joshua Moore and Helen Glasgow provided their best seller on personal and professional growth strategies as a gift for my readers.
Sign up here to get a free copy of the Growth Mindset book and more:
www.frenchnumber.net/growth

You may also like...
EMOTIONAL INTELLIGENCE SPECTRUM
EXPLORE YOUR EMOTIONS AND IMPROVE YOUR
INTRAPERSONAL INTELLIGENCE
BY JOSHUA MOORE AND HELEN GLASGOW

Emotional Intelligence Spectrum is the one book you need to buy if you've been curious about Emotional Intelligence, how it affects you personally, how to interpret EI in others and how to utilize Emotional Quotient in every aspect of your life.

Once you understand how EQ works, by taking a simple test, which is included in this guide, you will learn to harness the power of Emotional Intelligence and use it to further your career as you learn how to connect with people better.

You may also like...
I AM AN EMPATH
ENERGY HEALING GUIDE FOR EMPATHIC AND
HIGHLY SENSITIVE PEOPLE
BY JOSHUA MOORE

Am an Empath is an empathy guide on managing emotional anxiety, coping with being over emotional and using intuition to benefit from this sensitivity in your everyday life – the problems highly sensitive people normally face.

Through recongnizing how to control emotions you have the potential to make the most of being in tune with your emotions and understanding the feelings of people around you.

Begin your journey to a fulfilling life of awareness and support today!

You may also like...
MAKE ROOM FOR MINIMALISM
A PRACTICAL GUIDE TO SIMPLE AND SUSTAINABLE LIVING
BY JOSHUA MOORE

Make Room for Minimalism is a clear cut yet powerful, step-by-step introduction to minimalism, a sustainable lifestyle that will enable you to finally clear away all the physical, mental and spiritual clutter that fills many of our current stress filled lives. Minimalism will help you redefine what is truly meaningful in your life.

Eager to experience the world of minimalism?
Add a single copy of **Make Room for Minimalism** to your library now, and start counting the books you will no longer need!

FN№

Presented by French Number Publishing
French Number Publishing is an independent
publishing house headquartered in Paris, France
with offices in North America, Europe, and Asia.
FN№ is committed to connect the most promising
writers to readers from all around the world.
Together we aim to explore the most challenging
issues on a large variety of topics that are of
interest to the modern society.

FN№

Made in the USA
Monee, IL
20 February 2020